Cyber Citizenship and Cyber Safety™

Cyber Ethics

Diane Bailey

rosen publishing's
rosen
central®

New York

Published in 2008 by The Rosen Publishing Group, Inc.
29 East 21st Street, New York, NY 10010

Library of Congress Cataloging-in-Publication Data

Bailey, Diane.
Cyber ethics / Diane Bailey.—1st ed.
   p. cm.—(Cyber citizenship and cyber safety)
Includes bibliographical references and index.
ISBN-13: 978-1-4042-1349-4 (library binding)
1. Internet—Moral and ethical aspects—Juvenile literature.
2. Internet—Safety measures—Juvenile literature. 3. Online etiquette—
Juvenile literature. 4. Youth—Conduct of life—21st century—Juvenile
literature. I. Title. II. Title: Cyberethics.
TK5105.875.I57B338 2007
175—dc22

                                                    2007027291

Manufactured in Malaysia

Contents

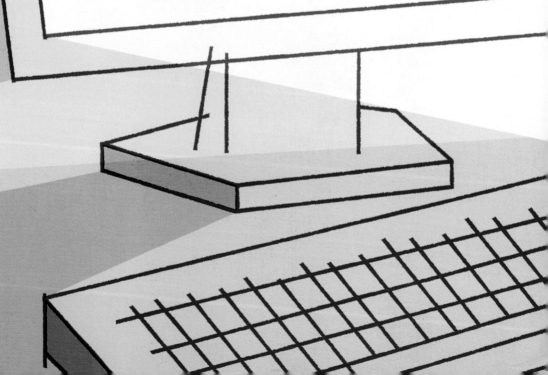

Introduction

Going on the Internet is like going to another world. You can find information for homework or play games. You can keep up with your favorite sports teams or write to the president of the United States. You can stay in touch with your friends or chat with people who like the same things you do.

This new world is big and may seem overwhelming. You might make a mistake without even knowing it. It's easy to use the Internet, but it's not always easy to do it right.

Ethics are the rules you use in life to help you decide what is right and wrong. Acting ethically means doing the right thing, sometimes in difficult situations. Cyber ethics is how you act when you are on the computer. Problems here are often similar to ones you've faced in real life. For example, if you take a CD from the store, it is stealing. If you download a song off the Internet without paying for it or without permission, that's considered by many people as being inappropriate and similar to stealing, particularly because there is no way to track how the creator of the song should get paid for his or her work. For others, this issue is debatable, and making a digital copy of a work is not considered stealing; however, it does not mean that you can use downloads to substitute for the commercial release of songs.

You have to think about other people's ethics, too. Giving your phone number to someone you've only met online is the same as giving it to a stranger. You don't know how that person might act.

The right thing to do offline is usually the right thing to do online. If you wouldn't do it face to face, don't do it on the computer.

Chapter 1

Becoming a Cyber Citizen

People who use the Internet make up the world's largest community. They come from different countries and cultures. Their religions or political opinions may be different from yours. They may have regular jobs or they may be brilliant scientists or celebrities. A boy from Nebraska could talk about global warming with an expert from India. You might not even know with whom you are talking! But remember, it's still a person at the other end.

Learning How to Act in Cyberspace

The way you treat people in cyberspace should be the same way you treat them in real life. However, cyberspace does create new situations. It can be confusing and difficult to see

These Chinese youths connect globally with
other Internet users by playing online games.

what the problems are. The consequences of your actions might
not be clear at first. You may have to think about a situation
differently from how you would think about it in real life.

For example, maybe a student at your school makes a Web
page and asks you to comment on girls in your class. You don't
like one of them and write something mean about her. By
insulting her in public, you can also get in trouble.

Suppose your friend buys a computer game and offers to let you copy it. At first, it sounds like a great deal. However, your friend only bought the right for one person to play that game. If he plays it, then he doesn't have the right to give it away, and you don't have the right to take it.

Life on the computer moves fast. You could be in trouble before you've had time to think about what you're doing. Maybe you get an e-mail that says "Free iPod!" That sounds good, but in the time it takes to click, you might let a harmful virus onto your computer.

Or, maybe your friend uses your computer and leaves her account logged in. With a few more clicks, you could invade her privacy by reading her e-mail.

Even if you act ethically, other people may not. Online "friends" may not be who they say they are. They may hide what they're trying to do. Unfortunately, adults sometimes hurt children they have contacted online. You have to protect your own privacy to stay safe. That's part of good cyber ethics.

Some people may have a different code of ethics. Hackers are people who break into computer systems. They often defend hacking because they say they can show where a computer system's security flaws are. However, hackers are going somewhere they have no right to be. This is unethical— and illegal.

At some point, you will have to decide for yourself what is right and what is wrong. If you are not sure, ask your parents, or use the "buddy system" and discuss it with a friend.

Talking over a problem can help you decide what to do.

The Trouble Spots

The places you can get into trouble on the Internet are often the same as in real life. For example, you know it would be wrong to read a letter your sister received. But if you read her e-mail, it's the same thing. You would think twice before saying something rude to someone in person. Doing it in an e-mail is called flaming—and it's still rude. If you copy information out of a book and pretend it's yours, it's called plagiarism. This is a form of cheating. Copying information off the Internet and using it as your own is also plagiarism. When you use someone else's work, you have to say where it came from unless it says it's OK not to give credit.

Kevin Mitnick *(right)* was arrested in 1995 for computer-related crimes and was imprisoned for five years. Hackers can go to jail for taking information or disrupting operations.

When you go onto the Internet, you can't see anyone, and no one can see you. You might feel as if no one knows who you are. You might think you can do something wrong and not get caught. But this is not true. There is technology

The Ten Commandments of Computer Ethics

- Don't use a computer to harm other people.
- Don't interfere with other people's computer work.
- Don't snoop around in other people's computer files.
- Don't use a computer to steal.
- Don't use a computer to lie.
- Don't copy or use software you haven't paid for, unless it says it's free.
- Don't use other people's computers without asking.
- Don't take words, pictures, or things created by someone else and use them as your own.
- Think about how your computer use affects other people.
- Always use computers in ways that are considerate and respectful of others.

(Adapted from the Computer Ethics Institute, Brookings Institution)

that can find out who you are and what you do online. And just because something's easy, it doesn't make it right.

People talk about being "online"—connected to the Internet. But good cyber ethics applies to any computer situation. For example, suppose you went onto your school's computer system to read students' grades. That would still be wrong even though the system is not connected to the Internet.

Nancy Willard is a teacher and author who writes about cyber ethics. She says students should put their actions to several tests:

The Golden Rule test: How would you feel if someone did the same thing to you?

The front page test: How would you feel if what you did was reported on the front page of the newspaper?

The mentor test: Think of someone you trust and respect. How would that person act? What would he or she think of what you are doing?

The real-world test: Compare your action to something similar in the real world. Would you still do it?

A Two-Way Street

Maybe you've heard the Internet called the "information superhighway." Like any road, the Internet goes two ways. A few years ago, people mostly used the Internet to get information. Now, they also use it to give information.

The term "Web 2.0" shows how people are more connected than ever. "Web" refers to the World Wide Web, the part of the Internet that lets users go to different sites. "2.0" means people are on the second version. In this new version, it's not just universities and companies that have Web sites. Lots of regular people have them, too. With profiles and blogs,

A Web 2.0 conference that was held in San Francisco, California, in 2006 drew people who wanted to learn more about how to communicate on the Internet.

people tell about themselves as well as find out about others. Also, they can comment on what they read. They are not just getting information off the Internet—they are putting it out there.

Being a responsible cybercitizen is also a two-way street. Nobody owns the Internet—not a person, or a company, or a country. The Internet is open to everyone. Everyone must help to keep it running smoothly.

Many schools have "Acceptable Use Policies." These explain how students can use the Internet at school. They say what types of sites students may visit, or to whom they can send e-mails. You might consider making rules to use at home, too. They can help you figure out what's OK, but no rule can cover every situation. It's important to use good judgment when it comes to being a smart cyber citizen.

Danger Ahead

G oing online can be risky. You can break the law, put yourself in danger, or hurt someone else. Often, you can't do something over. It's best to know what to do before you start.

Protecting Your Privacy

When you visit a Web site, you often give out information about yourself. For example, a game site might ask for your birth date. If you enter a contest or fill out a survey, you could list your address and telephone number.

You might ask, "So what? Does it matter if people know things about me?" Yes! Unethical people can use this information to hurt you. You have to protect yourself.

Chapter 2

Filters can help sort hundreds of unwanted spam e-mails into a separate folder in a mailbox.

You've probably gotten spam. These are e-mails that are sent to thousands of people at once. They may come from people or companies you don't know. Spam messages usually try to sell you something. Sometimes they are scams to trick you into sending money or giving out information about yourself. This is called phishing.

Opening spam can also let viruses or spyware onto your computer. Viruses are programs that hide in other programs and spread, just like a disease in your body. Some viruses will not harm your computer, but others cause serious damage. Spyware is a type of software that sneaks onto your computer and spies on you. It can find out what you do on the Internet and look at files stored on your computer. It can collect a lot of personal information.

With enough information, someone can pretend to be you. This is called identity theft. Usually, people do this to steal your money. Thieves often steal children's identities because children don't have credit problems. When someone falsely uses your name, it can hurt your reputation and cause problems in the future.

If you're not careful, you might invade someone else's privacy. If you give out a friend's e-mail address, she could start getting spam. Maybe it seems like a joke to pretend to be your brother and send e-mails from his account. It isn't a joke, though. It's a form of identity theft.

A popular way to use the Internet is to connect with other people. Maybe you write to people in chat rooms. Perhaps you have a profile on a social networking site like MySpace. You might have a blog where you keep an online journal or write about what you think on different issues.

Even if you don't use your real name online, it's easy to reveal a lot of information—maybe more than you should! Details add up. The name of your school, your age, and what things interest you all point to one person—YOU! If someone who finds you online can find you in real life, you could put yourself in danger.

Communicating Online

When you talk with someone face to face, you use more than words. Your tone of voice and body language add meaning to what you say. You also pick up on clues from other people. If your friend smiles, you know he understood your joke. If he looks away, you can guess that he's uncomfortable.

But in an e-mail or instant message (IM), you can't see or hear anything. You might write something you think is funny,

Cyber bullies use text messaging, instant messaging, and e-mail to send hurtful or threatening messages.

but the person reading it thinks you insulted him. If you receive an angry e-mail, you've been flamed! If you respond the same way, you might get into a flame war. These fights are online, but they are still real—and they still make people feel bad.

Do you like to forward jokes or send links to your favorite pages? Not everyone finds the same things funny or interesting. It's bad manners to fill up people's in-boxes or to send inappropriate things. Forwarding private e-mails is very bad manners.

One problem that children face is bullying. If you've been teased or harassed online, you've run into a cyber bully. Griefers are bullies who hang out at game sites. They cheat and gang up on other gamers.

During 2005–2006, the online safety organization i-Safe took a poll. It found that 22 percent of fifth- to twelfth-grade students knew someone who had been bullied online. Nineteen percent had said something hurtful themselves. It's OK to disagree with people, but it's not OK to insult or threaten them. It is unethical to write mean things about other students, your teachers, or your school. Doing so hurts people's feelings and their reputations.

Myths and Facts

Myth: Putting photographs on my Web site doesn't reveal any private information.

Fact: A picture shows what you look like, of course, but it may also have other clues about who you are. For instance, in the background there might be a soccer trophy with the name of your school.

Myth: I should reply to spam messages and ask the sender to stop.

Fact: Opening spam tells the sender you exist—and you'll probably end up getting more. Delete spam without opening it.

Myth: I bought software that lets me copy files from my friends' computers. Since I paid for this software, it's OK to copy songs my friends downloaded.

Fact: Peer-to-peer (P2P) software makes it easier to copy files, but it doesn't make it legal. Most songs must be paid for by each person.

Also, you could be the one who ends up looking bad. For example, imagine that your guidance counselor saw what you wrote. How about the family you babysit for? Remember, what you write online is more public than what you say in private. It's also more permanent. Things posted on the Internet can be found years later. Even private e-mail isn't always private. Someone might have saved or printed your message.

Sometimes it's fun to pretend to be someone else, but think carefully before you create a new identity online. If you lie about your age, you might get e-mails from adults you don't know. What if you said you were a doctor and someone asked you for advice? If pretending to be someone else could be harmful, then it's wrong.

Plagiarism and Illegal Downloading

With just a few clicks, you can find almost anything online. Suppose you are writing a report about Benjamin Franklin. It would be easy to copy information from the Internet into your own paper. If you were making a poster about gorillas, you might use pictures you found on a nature Web site. But you didn't write those words, and you didn't take those pictures.

Plagiarism is using someone else's work as your own. It doesn't matter if the information came from a book or off

The digital media player iTunes is a popular site for purchasing and downloading music.

the Internet. It's not fair to use other people's work without giving them credit. If you do, you can get in trouble.

Illegal downloading is another problem. With computers, it's easy to download songs or copy software. But if you don't pay for them, or have permission to use them for free, some people think it is inappropriate to download them. You are not taking a physical object, but you are taking the ability to listen to the song or use the software—and that doesn't belong to you. People who write songs and software make money only when people pay for the work. If everybody just took what they wanted, those people wouldn't have jobs. And if they stopped writing, you might never play a new game or listen to a new song. There are many circumstances, though, where downloading is entirely legal. For example, iTunes gives away a free song every week. Freeware is software that you don't have to pay for. It does depend on the circumstances that are involved, but if you download songs or copy software without stated permission and without paying the stated price, some people would argue that this action would be similar to stealing.

People—even young people—who commit online crimes can go to jail, pay fines, or lose their right to use the Internet. Their parents can get in trouble, too.

It might seem difficult to stay safe, legal, and nice on the Internet. But it isn't. Not if you learn how.

A Map for Cyberspace

Wouldn't it be great if cyberspace had a map? You'd never take a wrong turn—or if you did, you could easily go back. It isn't that easy, but there are some basic rules of the road. If you follow them, you can find your way without getting into trouble.

Staying Safe

When you ride in a car, you protect your body with a seat belt. When you surf the Internet, you should "buckle up" your privacy. You should never give personal information to someone you've met online. Remember that you also have a responsibility to keep your family's and friends' information private.

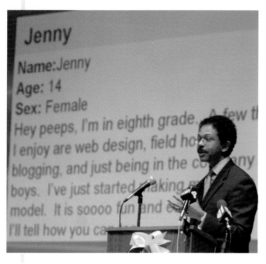

Peter C. Harvey, former attorney general of New Jersey, discusses Internet safety. "Jenny," the sender of the message behind him, was actually a middle-aged man.

Some adults use the Internet to harm children. The thought of online predators is scary, but you can learn to recognize the danger signs. When an adult tries to get close to a child, he does something called grooming. He may pretend that he is your age. He will try to earn your trust by asking lots of questions and pretending to care about you. If this happens to you, stop writing to this person and tell a trusted adult.

Cyber bullying is another problem. You can't make some-one act nice, but you can decide how to respond. Bullies want to upset you. If you react, they know it's working. Most bullies will give up if you ignore them. However, you may have to tell them to stop. Using monitored chat rooms and sites is a good idea. These sites have adults who look for problems and stop bad behavior.

If you run into griefers on a game site, stop playing the game for a while. Tell the people who run the game site. Some sites will let you create a private game where you play only with people you know.

Sometimes bullying goes a step further. Stalkers are people who refuse to leave you alone. They can be dangerous. If someone stalks you, save the messages and tell an adult.

Part of protecting yourself is protecting your computer, so make sure you have software that keeps out viruses and spyware. A pop-up blocker on your computer will help stop annoying ads.

Filters sort through information that enters and leaves your computer. By identifying certain keywords, filters can block Web sites that are meant only for adults. Outgoing filters can stop you from accidentally giving out personal information. And remember to back up your data regularly. Then, if you do have a problem, you won't lose everything!

Using the Internet for Schoolwork

The Internet is great for researching school projects. However, you still have to do your own work. It's unethical to plagiarize by copying things off the Internet and presenting them as your own. If you want to use a couple of sentences exactly the way you see them, put quotation marks around them and tell where you got them from. This is called fair use.

Remember that information on some Web sites can be misleading, incomplete, or false. It might even be harmful. Part of being ethical is being cyber literate. This means knowing how to evaluate information you find online. That way, you can avoid the bad stuff.

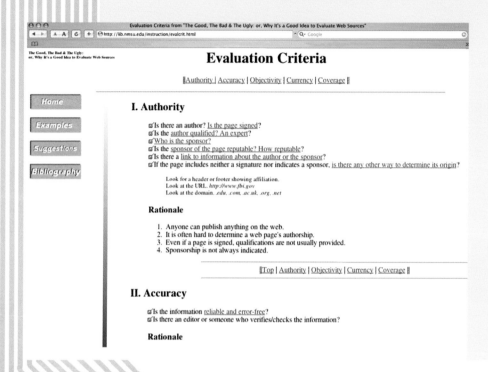

The New Mexico University State Library has a Web page (http://lib.nmsu.edu/instruction/evalcrit.html), created by Susan E. Beck, that lists criteria for evaluating a Web site, such as determining who created it and how accurate the site's information is.

People run Web sites for different reasons. Let's say you look up "dolphins." A university's job is to teach, so its Web site might have facts about dolphins. An environmental group might write about efforts to save dolphins in the wild. A company's Web site might sell clothing with pictures of dolphins. All of them come up when you search for "dolphins," but each site will have different information because it has a different purpose. Look at where information comes from, and then decide if it is useful. Your parents and teachers can help you choose good sites.

Netiquette

Put the words "network" and "etiquette" together, and you get "netiquette." The Internet is a huge network of people. Etiquette is good manners. "Netiquette" means using good behavior in cyberspace.

Writing e-mails can be tricky. Did you know that writing in all capital letters means you are shouting? Also, the same words can be interpreted different ways. Suppose you wrote, "That's crazy!" Someone could think that was an insult. Try putting a "smiley" at the end: "That's crazy! :-)" Then he will know you mean it in a good way. Emoticons such as "smileys" and "frownys" help you get the right meaning across.

Take time to reread an e-mail before you send it. You can correct any spelling mistakes, or rewrite something that sounds wrong. Avoid sending angry e-mails. Write one if it makes you feel better, but don't send it. Keep your messages clear and to the point, and don't use a lot of abbreviations and slang unless you know the other person will understand them.

Instant messages (IMs) are similar to e-mail, but they happen in real time, just like regular conversations. E-mails and instant messages aren't always the best ways to communicate.

:-) Smile

:-* Secret

:-O Surprised

:-@ Angry

:-(Sad

There are hundreds of emoticons, including those seen here, which can help add feelings to the words in an e-mail or instant message.

If you have something really important to say, you might want to say it in person.

Some of your online communication will be more public, so think about your "audience." If you join an online discussion group, you might want to "lurk" first. Read the messages without posting until you know how the group operates. And if you like to blog, keep in mind what people like to read. Don't write a lot of boring stuff about yourself. That doesn't make for interesting reading!

Trust Yourself

It may seem hard to remember all the rules of the road. The best plan is to trust yourself. Listen to your instincts. If it feels wrong, it probably is. If something makes you feel uncomfortable, tell someone. You are not being a tattletale. People who behave badly online should be stopped. You don't want yourself, someone in your family, or a friend to get hurt.

How to Create a Good Password

The job of a password is to protect your online accounts so that only you can get in. If you pick something easy to remember, like your name or phone number, it will also be easy for someone else to guess. A good password shouldn't point to who you are. It should be at least seven characters, and it should use both letters and numbers. Come up with a formula that you can remember. For example, you might use a word from the title of your favorite book, plus the month and day your parents were married. Think about creating a couple of passwords: one could be for game sites, and another could be for your e-mail account.

Your parents can help. They may know what to do when you don't. Also, let them know what you are doing online. Then they won't worry so much!

You will probably mess up at some point, even when you try not to. It's not unethical to make a mistake. Just try to correct it. For example, if you copy software without paying for it, go back and buy a legal copy. If you give out your friend's e-mail address, let her know so she can change it if necessary. And if you offend someone, apologize. That can save a lot of hurt feelings.

Chapter 4

The Real World

T hings that happen in cyberspace often have real-world
results. You can get in trouble at school or with the law
for things you did on the computer. Often it does not matter
if your action was an accident or a joke. The consequences
are the same.

Real Cases with Real Consequences

The news is full of stories about adults who hurt children
they met online. This is probably the worst thing that can
happen on the Internet, but other problems come up more
often. They can also have serious consequences.

Across the country, students who plagiarize are failing
classes. Students who write hurtful things—whether they

do it at school or from home—are being suspended or expelled. Some have been arrested.

Do you remember the movie *Star Wars*? In 2003, a teenager from Canada made a videotape. In the tape, he was having a lightsaber fight with a pretend enemy. Nobody else was supposed to see the tape, but some other students from his school found it and posted it on the Internet. The boy was teased so much he dropped out of school and had to see a psychiatrist.

A twelve-year-old girl from New York City downloaded songs off the Internet. She used file-sharing (peer-to-peer) software that her mother had bought. But she didn't pay for the songs themselves. The Recording Industry Association of America (RIAA) is a group that represents people in the music business. They sued the twelve-year-old! The girl said she did not know she had done anything illegal because her mother had paid for the software. It didn't matter. Her mother had to pay $2,000. In other cases, people have had to pay more.

In Boston, a fifteen-year-old boy sent threatening e-mails to a school. He also hacked into the computers at the telephone company. He cut off the phones to hundreds of people. When he was caught, a judge sent him to a juvenile detention facility. Of course, he also lost his Internet access.

You may do something that's legal, but it can still backfire. Two college swimmers in Louisiana criticized their coach online. They got kicked off the team. Other students have been turned down for jobs because their future bosses

Authorities questioned teenager Julia Wilson *(left)* after she posted a threatening message to President George W. Bush on MySpace.

didn't like things they had written online.

Taking Action

Keeping children safe on the Internet is a big concern. The government has passed laws to try to protect children. The Child Online Protection Act (COPA) was supposed to stop children from going to harmful Web sites. This meant the Web sites had to find out how old their users were. But in March 2007, a judge ruled that this law was unconstitutional. He said it could invade people's privacy and limit their rights to free speech.

Another law, the Children's Online Privacy Protection Act (COPPA), is designed to protect children's personal information. It limits what information Web sites can get from children who are under the age of thirteen, and parents have to say it's OK.

The law doesn't always work. In September 2006, the social networking site Xanga was fined $1 million. It had let children younger than thirteen years old sign up without their parents' permission. In this case, users had admitted they

Hackers and Crackers

In books and movies, hackers—people who break into computer systems—are often heroes. They use their special skills to save the day. Many hackers think what they do is good. They say that hacking shows where a computer system has weaknesses. Sometimes they think of themselves as watchdogs. For example, hackers might break into a company's computer system. If they believe the company is doing something wrong, the hackers will catch them.

Hackers say it is "crackers" who cause real trouble. Crackers break into systems because they want to do something bad. A hacker might break into a school's computer system just to prove that he can. A cracker would do something wrong once he was inside, such as change students' records.

Even if it's not "cracking," hacking is still unethical because the hackers don't have the right to be inside the computer system. Hackers have a lot of technical skill, but many companies will not hire them. They don't trust them.

were too young. However, children can lie about their age. This makes it hard to enforce the law.

Social networking sites like Xanga and MySpace get a lot of attention. Children often give out personal information on these sites and put their safety at risk.

A new law was suggested in March 2007. Under this law, social networking sites would have to verify the ages of people who sign up. This can be difficult, however.

Government agencies such as the Cyber Crime Unit of the Mississippi attorney general's office work with teens to teach them how to protect themselves against online predators.

Children younger than seventeen often do not have proof of their age, such as a driver's license.

MySpace recently announced a new software program for parents. The program shows parents what age and town their children list in their profiles. But, they can't look at any personal messages. The program helps parents find out whether their children are misrepresenting themselves. At the same time, it protects children's privacy. However, many people—including lawmakers—say this is not enough. There is still much controversy about rules and laws for social networking sites.

Using Computers for Good

Good cyber ethics is a lot about not doing the wrong thing. You can also use the Internet to do the right thing.

An activist is someone who works for a certain cause. A cyber activist works by using the Internet. Do you want to save the rainforest? Feed hungry people? Support a candidate for president? On the Internet, you can learn about different issues. You can decide which ones interest you. Then you can figure out how to get involved. For example, if you are concerned about the environment, you might learn how to start a recycling program at your school.

The Internet can reach all kinds of people in all kinds of places. In the past, you needed to have some technical knowledge to create a Web site. Now, there are easy ways to do it. You do not need to have special skills. You can make a Web site about the things you believe in.

Another thing you can do is to post your writing or art on the Web. This is a good way to express yourself. It also helps remind you to respect other people's creations. That's your work out there. How would you feel if someone took it without asking you or giving you credit? Remember, if you want your work to be used by other people, you can always give permission!

Students at a Texas junior high school had a good idea. They drew small pictures to create their own clip art library and posted them on the Web. Then they signed forms that said the pictures were free for anyone to use. Students and teachers at the school used them in projects, handouts, and the school newspaper.

Positive actions like these are a great way to learn about how to use the Internet—and you can do good in the real world at the same time!

Chapter 5

A Changing Future

W eb 2.0 is already here. Who knows when people will be talking about Web 3.0? Computers and the Internet are always changing. Problems people face now may not be around in a few years. But there will be new ones to deal with.

New Issues and New Approaches

New technology can solve some problems. New laws can punish criminals. But no problem has a single answer that always works. Sometimes the "solution" only creates a new ethical problem. For example, at some schools, officials can read the e-mails students send. If the e-mails could hurt someone else, the officials can stop them from going out. However, some people argue that no one should be able to

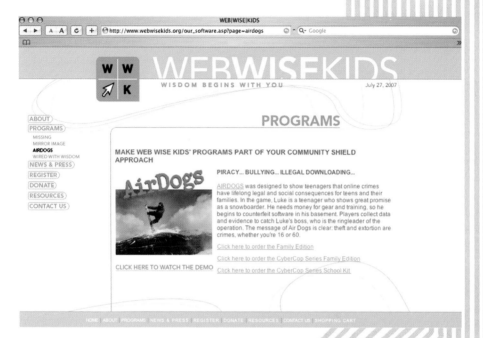

There are organizations that teach teens about the legal and social consequences of online crimes. One example is the group WebWiseKids (www.webwisekids.org) and its game AirDogs, which teaches users about ethical computer use.

read or stop someone else's e-mails. They say it invades their privacy and takes away their right to free speech. Who is right? Sometimes there is no clear answer. Cases like these are being discussed in court.

Teaching people to act smart can keep them from getting in trouble in the first place. In 2006, the state of Virginia passed new laws about how students could use the Internet at school. Besides the rules for using the Internet, an important part of the law was that schools had to teach students about how to use the Internet.

Some companies and organizations, such as the organization WebWiseKids (www.webwisekids.org), have created games to teach young people about ethical issues. One game is based on a real case of a teenager who copied software and sold it for extra money. Another game puts children in the middle of a cyber crime. They can play a hacker, a victim, or an FBI agent. In the games, students make decisions and then deal with the consequences—just like in real life.

A Clean Slate

Some computer scientists have started talking about a new Internet. They want to stop using the Internet that exists now. They want to start over with a whole new system. It would be a clean slate.

When the Internet began, the people who used it were a small group. Many of them knew each other. They did not need to keep the Internet secure or private. Now, millions of people use the Internet. Privacy has become a big problem. If people do not have enough privacy on the Internet, they won't want to use it. On the other hand, if it is too easy to hide who you are, it makes it hard to find people who are causing trouble.

The National Science Foundation (NSF) is an independent agency within the U.S. government. One of its aims is to support people who look for ways to fix problems involving the use of the Internet. The NSF also promotes the use of good ethics on the Internet. One of the NSF's goals is to encourage the use of the Internet for "social good." This means helping all of society. For example, putting emergency weather reports online would be one way to assist everyone. Being able to reach 911 from a computer would be another benefit.

Right now, the Internet is like the world's biggest democracy. It's open to everyone. Everyone is equal. Sometimes you might go to a game site run by a big company. Other times, you might visit your friend's personal Web page. Either way, it takes about the same amount of time to get there.

However, some people want to control traffic on the Internet. They want to decide what information goes first and how fast it travels. If these people don't think some information is important, it might have to stay in the slow lane.

Many people do not like this idea. They say the ethical thing to do is to keep the Internet neutral. No place would be the favorite. No piece of information would always get to be first in line. It wouldn't matter what it was or who asked for it.

The First Line of Defense

The current generation of young people has been called Generation @. This name comes from e-mail addresses. Suppose your address is yourname@cyberethics.com. If you say it out loud, it sounds like this: "Your name at cyber ethics dot com."

YouTube and CNN hosted a debate among Democratic presidential hopefuls and broadcast it online in July 2007 to involve young people in national politics.

You are growing up with technology your parents didn't have. For example, your generation made presidential debate history when you submitted video questions for the U.S. presidential candidates via YouTube in debates hosted by the popular video sharing Web site and the Cable News Network (CNN) in 2007. You may know more than your parents do about computers. The good news is, many adults know that they can learn from young people.

Companies such as Microsoft and Walt Disney sometimes ask young Web users for advice. If they are creating

Students into Teachers

Who's the expert? When it comes to teaching online safety and ethics to students, sometimes other students make the best teachers. The safety organization i-Safe has a program called i-Mentors. Students take online classes to learn about safety. They share the information in schools and can get school credit for their activities.

Another organization, WiredSafety, has a group called Teenangels. Students who are between the ages of thirteen and eighteen can join. They also have Tweenangels, for children who are nine to twelve years old. Internet experts and FBI officers teach these students how to use the Internet safely. The "Angels" then teach other students.

Teenangel chapters can focus on their particular interests. For example, some might work with law enforcement agencies, such as the Federal Bureau of Investigation (FBI), to learn how they deal with online crimes. In turn, Angels teach officers how teens act online—from using slang to chatting about rock bands. That way, officers can pretend to be teens when they're looking for online predators. Other Teenangel groups might explore how different cultural groups in the United States use the Internet. Understanding people's different attitudes can make going online a better experience.

The Internet joins traditional libraries as a valuable research tool.

a new game, they find out what the players think about it and how challenging it is to play, among other issues. Children know first-hand what aspects of the game might be problematic. One group "test-drove" a Disney game site. It recommended a change to protect younger children, and Disney ended up making that change.

In the last decade, the Internet has become a part of many people's lives. It's almost hard to imagine an "offline" life. But the Internet comes with its own set of problems. It probably always will. That does not mean you should avoid the Internet. It just means you should learn to deal with the ethical issues you face. Fortunately, coping with a situation is less confusing and scary if you are prepared. If you have edu-cated yourself about the kinds of problems that can happen, you will know what to do if they occur.

Remember that whether you are using the Internet at school or at home, or whether you are by yourself or with your family or friends, it's up to you to make good choices. The first line of defense is yourself.

Glossary

blog An abbreviation of "Weblog;" an online journal, diary, or commentary about different issues.

chat room A place where people gather online to talk in real time.

cracker Someone who breaks into computer systems in order to do something harmful.

cyber literacy Knowing how to evaluate and use information found online.

cyberspace The online world and its activities.

emoticon A symbol used in e-mails that represents a specific feeling or tone.

filter A type of software that analyzes and sorts information sent and received online.

flame An angry or insulting message.

griefers Online bullies on game sites.

grooming When an adult establishes a bond of trust with a child, with an intent to harm.

hacker Someone who breaks into computer systems.

mentor A person who is admired and respected.

netiquette Proper manners for online communication.

peer-to-peer software Also called P2P or file-sharing software; a type of software that lets one computer exchange information or files with another computer, without going through a central computer.

phishing An online scam in which someone sends e-mails asking for people's personal information. The e-mails appear to come from legitimate companies but are actually fake.

plagiarism Using someone else's creative work without giving credit for it.

predator Someone who hurts or takes advantage of others.

social networking site A site where people create profiles and connect with each other online.

spam Unwanted e-mail sent to a lot of people at once.

spyware A type of software that secretly collects information.

stalking Refusing to leave someone alone.

virus A type of program that hides inside another program and duplicates itself, often causing problems on computers.

For More Information

CyberWise (National Strategy for the Protection of Children
   from Sexual Exploitation on the Internet)
155 Queen Street, 8th Floor
Ottawa, ON K1A OH5
Canada
(800) 622-6232
Web site: http://www.cyberwise.ca
   This Canadian organization provides information and resources for
   using the Internet safely.

Internet Keep Safe Coalition
5220 36th Street North
Arlington, VA 22207
(866) 794-7233
E-mail: info@iKeepSafe.org
Web site: http://www.iKeepSafe.org
   This organization teaches basic Internet safety through games and
   other activities.

i-SAFE, Inc.
5900 Pasteur Court, Suite 100
Carlsbad, CA 92008
(760) 603-7911
E-mail: media@isafe.org
Web site: http://www.isafe.org
   This company operates programs that help youths learn to take
   control of their Internet use in safe, legal ways.

NetSmartz Workshop
Charles B. Wang International Children's Building
699 Prince Street
Alexandria, VA 22314-3175
(800) 843-5678
E-mail: NetSmartz_Contact@ncmec.org
Web site: http://www.netsmartz.org
NetSmartz Workshop is cosponsored by the National Center for Missing and Exploited Children and the Boys & Girls Clubs of America to provide information on Internet safety.

WebWiseKids
P.O. Box 27203
Santa Ana, CA 92799
(866) WEBWISE (932-9473)
E-mail: info@webwisekids.org
Web site: http://www.webwisekids.org
WebWiseKids is an organization that specializes in preventing online child victimization through simulation games in classrooms.

Web Sites

Due to the changing nature of Internet links, Rosen Publishing has developed an online list of Web sites related to the subject of this book. This site is updated regularly. Please use this link to access the list:

http://www.rosenlinks.com/cccs/cyet

For Further Reading

Farnham, Kevin, and Dale Farnham. *MySpace Safety: 51 Tips for Teens and Parents*. Pomfret, CT: How-To Primers, 2006.

Gordon, Sherri Mabry. *Downloading Copyrighted Stuff from the Internet: Stealing or Fair Use?* Berkeley Heights, NJ: Enslow Publishers, Inc., 2005.

Gosney, John W. *Blogging for Teens*. Boston, MA: Thomson Course Technology PTR, 2004.

Herumin, Wendy. *Censorship on the Internet: From Filters to Freedom of Speech*. Berkeley Heights, NJ: Enslow Publishers, Inc., 2004.

MacDonald, Joan Vos. *Cybersafety: Surfing Safely Online*. Berkeley Heights, NJ: Enslow Publishers, Inc., 2001.

McCarthy, Linda. *Own Your Space: Keep Yourself and Your Stuff Safe Online*. Upper Saddle River, NJ: Addison-Wesley, 2006.

Menhard, Francha Roffé. *Internet Issues: Pirates, Censors and Cybersquatters*. Berkeley Heights, NJ: Enslow Publishers, Inc., 2001.

Schwartau, Winn. *Internet & Computer Ethics for Kids*. Seminole, FL: Interpact Press, 2001.

Spangenburg, Ray, and Kit Moser. *Savvy Surfing on the Internet: Searching and Evaluating Web Sites*. Berkeley Heights, NJ: Enslow Publishers, Inc., 2001.

Willard, Nancy E. *Computer Ethics, Etiquette & Safety for the 21st-Century Student*. Eugene, OR: International Society for Technology in Education, 2002.

Bibliography

Angwin, Julia. "MySpace Moves to Give Parents More Information." *Wall Street Journal.* January 17, 2007. Retrieved April 15, 2007 (http://online.wsj.com/public/article/SB11690073358797862 5-TzfakoF_hN6f6R45g_cLsm3OJZ0_20080116.html).

Baard, Mark. "NSF Preps New, Improved Internet." *Wired.* August 26, 2005. Retrieved April 20, 2007 (http://www.wired.com/science/ discoveries/news/2005/08/68667).

Cable in the Classroom. "Digital Ethics." Retrieved April 5, 2007 (http://www.ciconline.org/digitalethics).

Harris, Frances Jacobson. *I Found It on the Internet: Coming of Age Online.* Chicago, IL: American Library Association, 2005.

Johnson, Doug. *Learning Right from Wrong in the Digital Age: An Ethics Guide for Parents, Teachers, Librarians and Others Who Care About Computer-Using Young People.* Worthington, OH: Linworth Publishing, Inc., 2003.

Kornblum, Janet, and Mary Beth Marklein. "What You Say Online Could Haunt You." *USA Today.* March 8, 2006. Retrieved April 15, 2007 (http://www.usatoday.com/tech/news/internetprivacy/2006-03-08-facebook-myspace_x.htm).

Magid, Larry, and Anne Collier. *MySpace Unraveled: What It Is and How to Use It Safely.* Berkeley, CA: Peachpit Press, 2007.

McGee, Marianne Kolbasuk. "Kids Put Online Safety First." *Information Week.* July 4, 2005. Retrieved April 14, 2007 (http://www. informationweek.com/showArticle.jhtml?articleID=164904402).

Starr, Linda. "Tools for Teaching Cyber Ethics." *Education World.* Retrieved April 6, 2007 (http://64.233.167.104/search?q= cache:0sOODXZ4qMEJ:www.educationworld.com/a_tech/ tech/tech055.shtml).

Willard, Nancy E. *Cyber-Safe Kids, Cyber-Savvy Teens: Helping Young People Learn to Use the Internet Safely and Responsibly.* San Francisco, CA: Jossey-Bass, 2007.

Index

About the Author

Diane Bailey grew up in a family whose members were on the cutting edge of computer technology. Her house was the first on the street with a personal computer—and for a long time, it was the only one. Now, her home has four computers, nine e-mail addresses, and two children, so she knows how important it is to have a plan for using technology—even when that technology is always changing. A former newspaper reporter, Bailey now writes on a variety of nonfiction topics.

Photo Credits:

Cover Les Kanturek; pp. 7, 12, 19, 22, 30, 32 © AP Images; p. 9 © J Bounds-RNO/Corbis Sygma; p. 14 © www.istockphoto.com/ Yong Hian Lim; p. 16 © John Birdsall/The Image Works; p. 24 Susan Beck, from *The Good, The Bad & The Ugly: or, Why It is a Good Idea to Evaluate Web Sources*, 1997; p. 40 © ColorBlind Images/Getty Images.

Editor: Kathy Kuhtz Campbell; **Photo Researcher:** Cindy Reiman